dreamland

trash

Saint Julian Press
Poetry

PRAISE for *dreamland trash*

This is the opposite of a sophomore slump. Like the latest subatomic experiments in above-the-speed-of-light velocity, for a fraction of a second, when the same particle is in two places at the same time, Dylan Krieger will be there and elsewhere. As if *Giving Godhead* weren't good enough, suddenly she hits out past light-years of stratospheres and reproductive insanities of biology back to the "invertebrate mother" and the lunacy of a planet organized largely around humanoid self-destruction. The scale becomes both precise and enormous, echoes of things heard as if through water in a glass. You will have to think about the sound of it all for a few days, it is both so familiar and so volatile. *dreamland trash* is one of the most perfect IED's ever made.

Thomas Simmons
NOW

"Holding whole generations up at sexpoint," *dreamland trash* is ingenious, witty, and electric. We are just as likely to wake up next to a moaning unicorn as we are to be abducted by deranged YouTube automatic captions. It's in this derangement that we begin to see the late-capitalist world inside out and upside down, for its cheap thrills and absolute devaluation of the self. Abandon and alienation are rendered in a linguistically dense, gothic style, deeply aware of the "day-glo chokehold" we are all in.

Sandra Simonds
Further Problems with Pleasure, Steal It Back

dreamland trash

Dylan Krieger

Published by
SAINT JULIAN PRESS, Inc.

2053 Cortlandt, Suite 200

Houston, Texas 77008

www.saintjulianpress.com

ISBN-13: 978-0-9986404-4-0

ISBN: 0-9986404-4-1

Library of Congress Control Number: 2017956190

Cover Art: Rachel Krieger © 2017

Cover Design: Ron Starbuck

Author Photo Credit: Blair Thompson

For the United States
under my bedsheets

the United States that
coughs all night and

won't let me sleep

CONTENTS

medicine manhole

sayonara, serotonin!

draw one // pick again

i collect your blood   so i can lose it

although my ideal mate will always be

a morphine drip   i'm scoping out

potential callers w/ my radar gun aflutter

press on my   robot fontanel &

watch my gears grind underwater

the sea belongs   to absent fathers

an utmost lonely bound by lo-fi

acrimony   the aches & moans

that make us itch for broken bones

so many   molotov cocktails

i confused w/ mazel tov

so many silly   awkward pauses

i could have been filling up

w/ dopamine   & frantic gaud

automatomic

there will one day come a cataclysm where everyone will turn

magically oyster—*oy vey* my own private apocalypse blitz

a pox upon the lips of latin fiends full of disease

the master race is still unclean

feel free to stay awhile & watch me

light my phantom limbs on fire

a whole new rite of *woe is me!*

i'm fully gaud & fully man-eating

fully hamburger pasties & gnostic lobotomy

believe me, my inner parking lot is filled w/

lost kittens stitching cancer symptoms to their paw pads

we are all so balls-out desperate to leak the clean stuff instead of

this murk shit cut with baby lax & groupon shopping sprees

lick the dirt out of my spray-tan creases, beam me up to

newfound statistics of thunder & sleet, then add cream

i am the curdled tissues you decipher

when the goats bleat out their night-song

i am the underwater crucible

who shows you its back-fins flash sheen

i'm still stripping my barbies naked

just to see how far they'll let me take it

stay put & feel my stubby fingers fumble for locked doors

i'm forming puddles but where I come from

no one mops me off the floor

ghost porn

despite the sting of solar vision

i still self-identify as a child vampire

holding whole generations up at sexpoint

no golden winner   only silver indecision

when the city streets ran out of strippers

we cat-called the river: *hey sexy!* big muddy

shakes its ass out to sea sick w/ dredgers & jumpers

what's one more corpse on the forklift the stork

swallows for breakfast? i'm all for crying out *where*

wolf or congenital warp   libeling the only viral shine that

spreads us too thin at night between setoff warning lights

& buckets of nothing but the dust we become under history's

thumbnail gif: an imperial conquest surprise-ending in

faceplant instant replaying forevery eternity squared or

divided by zero   *in the face of pain there are no heroes*

but out here in the flyover states both stay stuck in a riddle

UFO

this lobotomy is getting the worst of me. so frisky in high heels and leather, i barely even notice the shiv muzzle quivering in the corner of my eye-hole. please fuck me up with god-knows-what. i'm a thief, i'm a slut, i'm stealing your wallet as we speak in the dusk and go loping through prairies with snails in our guts. i dig you with a special kind of sucker punch. when we dove off the dock, we realized the whole lakefront was spiked with rum and fish spunk. well so what. when we run out of fun stuff to thrum it's just humdrum mitosis and satellite drones on and on. the sea is full of nasty hazard rot and whatever shot at collective unconscious we've got is not stopping our lot from not stopping to gather moss on its way to extinctive forgot, where the new hot marketing demographic's called DOOM and they can't wait to see what the free market's got up its skirt like a circus tent thumping in time to the sound of new mothers disclosing their cudgels and luring their babes on to alien abduction goodbyes

borderline

i'm the borderline hoarder bored gargoyles come quick to haunt
w/ their crouching hindquarters

in the attic dust, i'm not afraid to say i found an alien musk that
sent me undressing my ancestors

one by one into ovens of rust—here's your bundled lump sum:
crunch the numbers down &

ground them into backhands of rabid distrust. on the path back to
straight & near-loved, i wake

up in a day-glo chokehold while the nightclub goes up in smoke-
rings out the top. what a

triumphal human test-drive: to spy your former selves
dismembered by the karmic wheel of

arson—whether biblical damnation be a fable or a forecast, i'm
counting myself able to reform

my heathen ways by dry-heaving my way into america's heart-
seams: borderline states of a

borderline emergency, borderline requiring triple bypass
surgery—and the borderline real & the

borderline dream share a j on the street where they're borderline
free from all the seething

vows of vengeance the sea sucks through its teeth, like a family
man stubbing his terminal daze

on disease: the hunched statues all see it, but they're not sure
which potion to drink to piss clean

pater // pattern

at night i try to trace a pattern in your hands that might explain
their villainy

but all i find is last night's bar stamp and a set of freckles
mimicking a fox head

so when i fall asleep i dream that a mechanic-caller in a fox mask
murders me

then sends me soaring out a window with eyes already fixed &
violating

like vertigo in guernica, my dying hovers overhead, projected
onto cubist fruits

that fast abstract me out of bed—to take a piss, the hardwood
floor elaborates

on what you haven't said, directs all wayward toes toward water
harps on its

slackness at the jamb—and by the time i'm back i'm elsewhere
floating

somewhere underground, thinking in click habits (i.e.
relationships & outer space)

as if my cyber-sphere is every-here, but suddenly i'm treading
water in a sea as

deep as grief, and america asks, *who is that alligator lying waiting
underneath?*

but if the monster is to kill me, what's the point in all this dread?
why don't i

paint a blueprint in these pruney flesh folds for him to codify to
shreds?

un-song

call me humpty cum dumpster

no one can put me back together

but they can fuck the pieces

listen to my loss for words

suspend me hypothetically

in a brain-vat of my own

unmaking, stating telepathy

only confirms my prior

suspicion that according to

autocorrect i'm ducking

shivs right and left, waking up

drowning in a pool of my own

sonnet, wherein the only volta

is my baby blackout crowning

and hey, there's nothing half-

way nice to say about

a breach as freak as that

sympathy pill

tucked up inside your blood

brain barrier

i can steer diff types of craze

heinous holesaws

hissing quick memory

loss & *sayonara,*

serotonin! you'll never under-

stand the stratosphere

of saturn: some sacred circle

permanent enough to

deck in rings & silver wormholes

such signals on the skin

open a portal to the skull's

faint oscillate

from basehead angels all the way

to dilettantes

still safe to say even satan himself

can't date-rape

the willing villain who drinks his

antifreeze neat

if your radiator is my afterlife

vibration maybe

suicide's not all that sad, just

something swinging

overhead that can't comedown

breeders

now that my number   of sexual pardons

is high enough   to buy itself a drink

it's going sober   for the first time

since my first time   pinned under a

rainspout spreading   viral *red-*

redone- redundancy   like a leopard

fighting leprosy   *same rat, different hat*

carbon copies double   dating each other

making babies via inter   sexting x & y axes

half lamb's fleece   half plaster cast out

stalemating to dry   my rapist got whiskey

dick so we just shot   the shit inside our heads

knocked another bottle back   chose death instead

committed

today i googled   *how to get committed*

        as if a wedding   dress & medic's

coat were cut out   from the same un-cloth:

        bobbin full of fairy   dust & buckles latch

at *watch your back*   a riddle where you lose your

        head but grow a   golden shell against your

every former self   w/ one priest

        in one tomb   i thee woo

using this sparkly   superstition metronome *click*

        b/c there is no   going home for

little fickle aliens   padding their cells w/

        space age anomalies   like optional sex organs or

chernobyl drone porn   let's consummate

        our stakeout vows   by dying on

this dotted line   slice here and here

        and then rewind   to a time when mom

& dad staked all the   vampires outside

    walked their own sanity   lines down the mirror

which made the house   hum like a fuselage

    finding its underside   no longer tied to the night

over[h]eating

sucking on a handicap sign in the street shine, my empathy muscle starts to burn blue. who are all these passersby, mummified by layers of vitamite mayo and bi-weekly payrolls? once, when i was only two, i gulped down too many special interest groups and got sick on their pharmacy stew. my mother brought me the bucket, but i refused it. i preferred their excretions to leak down my forefront real formal. i preferred the bare brute of ruin, like full frontal surgery. i've never understood john wayne masculinity. what's manlier than braving a forthright exchange w/ your own demon babies, cracking at their softy head seams? they've been speaking in turns since the day you were born, egging on your unconscious under brimstony seethes of unseen. speak back, and they just might let you muzzle mother's hungry cudgel. speak now, or forever molt your meat.

un-cudgel

where there's a spine
there's a gutter

like misery & cream
cheese we

fit together held by
sex & letters

one after another i
smother my

stuttered affections
for those w/o

rubbers or the power
to un-cudgel

their inner mothers
look out i'm

outing everyone i've
never been

allowed to love

snorting bad

fortune & some fat-ass

line about

abortion-laced buffets

teaching portion

control to americans

who still breed

& feed in boldface

uppercase outrage

against the day that

prays backspace

efface their kind like

spermicide

designed to wipe the

ripe world

out to sea

poison fog

exactly how long does one wait before telling their exterminator
they've ingested tenfold the suggested dose of whatever that
termite tank holds? in but a moment, i'll be bat-shit crash-
landing on a planet no one should ever call home. show me my
starship captain's made of foam. against my internal go-getter's
better judgment, i'm stop-motion slow-going it alone all the way
down memory road. my scarecrow stalemate w/ an overhead
drone turned out to be more than just phone taps & doggy-style
burial zones. the trauma tooth loosens, and i'm back in the
phallic fun house of my youth skin, where i found all my friends
were imaginary menageries of *no*. stuffed full of called bluffs and
all history's haystacks emitting their high-stakes enormity smoke,
i know entropy is still widely misunderstood, but it really does
make us blow colder, like a porcupine shedding its spiny surprise
in the hides of the violently born, we spike our predators' gene
pools w/ poisonous thorns & the neighborhood hooch cooked up
by a coroner—imagine a tepid liquid heating up w/o end, w/o
borders. imagine no more vultures. i'm still thinking though
brainless: *hey you* in the straw head, tell me your life story—or
would it burden you too much to outburst your already-stressed
seams for a foreigner's curse of hurt-hoarding?

caption this conspiracy

far cry

a far cry from full tide. a far cry from curtain & cord. a fist full of quick tinsel. a fuck ton of lost fur. he said, *are you wearing spurs?* i said, *no, but i've a belt made of blacksmiths.* yes, all the blacksmiths i have blown. all the blacksmiths i have heated up/hammered/burst/beaten into gold. they are a hoard of a thousand horses, mounting fire in the dust. they flagellate their bellies to burlap, they scrape their fat faces to fringe. i mean to say: i pricked them with a nasty nettle, or, i packed in their pistols with clay. either way, they are made to push up my marina body. either way, i am full of mad boats. they are walked on by the far cries of the drowning in the harbor towns. they are burnt by the search lights in the bay. there is a prize in my navel for the one who swallows the largest electric eel. there is a button. a kettle. a basket of bruised fruit. there is a locket with a picture of a peasant penetrating a lighthouse, his hind haunch to the sea, in the shadow of a fish-filled wave

disappearing act

the one thing you
        can't forget is that
you can't remember

how the bullet stopped
        the perp surrendered
his seed to the sheet

instead of filling his
        victim's ink— *well what
the hell?* we all fall down

like forestry thru history
        in timelapsed saturnalia
a tapestry of macro-failure

wherein the only sordid
        storm clouds left leave
chemtrails tracing your

name across the ozone
        layer: matricidal sideshow
nosediving a diamond

proposal to no one
        in three-ring kiss cam

super fluids

tonight the heavens tried a
devil's threesome: two
moons at once

and we wonder why fetuses
keep falling out of
the newspaper

the view to my insides is
live streaming down
the dead's throat

how's that for reverse
cannibal? caverns
of never

forlorning w/ tweaker
perfume & capped
ventricles

the senator says it all:
lemme emotionless
grab a vote

a rude quote from the

cleanup crew shuts

background

sounds out *am-ne-si-a*

like *am-ni-ot-ic*

only

temporary side effects

scoring more & more

trap doors

call your dealer if you begin

to feel an apocalyptic

thud b/c you

might be blasting off to planet

clutch: homo sapie's

achy breaky

last-ditch dud

ET proletariat

above a diff fat-cat planet ships keep busy
listing mammalian inventory of lip service

moths communicate via meme device
fuck goes the tooth fairy, this is real life

a knife-fight featuring non-stick agnostics
& sparkly juveniles shredding their rebel

files all a-smile: *beam me up* the solid-works
technologies of their optic mitosis, foaming

armatures pre-formed w/ built-in information
nozzle, spraying *we grovel to make ourselves*

gravel—god save the hive mind that splits the
cliff into pebbles! well I'd settle for a dental

plan or storied cure to the common probe
no need to revere a clearance level or bevel

one's natural bacteria into dreamland trash
in time our downwind adapters grow inter

galactic & gorge on red atmospheres oozing

florescence, ecstatic in germ & in bribe

congenital warp

the golden hour has a hole in it

when i'm left home alone all the saints fall off the walls

the phone taps trickle out their paranormal paranoia

this time a divining rod rubs wrong

msg heard round the world

god only knows

        how he planned to

announce the end

        times before telephones

or twitter terrorism

        how bout we go back

to that jurassic

        backdrop where if the

whole world heard

        one person speak he's

like obvi a deity

        no newsroom to hijack

at high noon or

        brand-spanked remote

explosives synced

        to trigger others overseas

we earthlings

        need our limits *please*

stop this whole

        violent villain takeover

before the coast

        lines start to give way

to some final tidal

                wave   escape their

own live sacrifice

                by drowning every

goddamn spambot

                web server & w/ them

little human race

                a cautionary tale for

neighbor aliens

                to air thru space

electric lineage

btwn fact & fan fic
i'll boo who? all the
little ppl, gray & blue
a new world order of u-
nited star boards means
to end our borders EARTH
LINGS, sordid orphans of
antiquity, are you even sry
you sacrificed mommy &
daddy to the godheads of
industry? you're pissing oil
down their headstones in a
dream daze when you hear
you wet the bed, son, waking
up to mess & metaphor all
mixed together in your head
unsettling down to its very
bacterial spread: amoebae have
no family values so they just
split apart, fuck off sans dread
b/c sometimes it's better to be
dead than hunting boogeymen
too busy splashing black holes
into their hand-me-down

gene pools or pawning

whatever's left under

the sediment unsaid

absence knows best

false eyes
found me out

i skin my rhyme
scheme from the ass down
rub a nickel

do a butterfly dive
outta the kitchen sink
when i was five
i burned my hymen
on a hanging

chandelier perhaps
half glass coffin
the only part i still
remember is the
part that fell away
btwn the heretical sheets
writhing like a centipede

ablaze in my ongoing
blazon about you i
say you're more
ram than lamb
more horny satanic
bleached rind on
the brambled path back
to unrighteous unconscious

i'm mixing myths again
but somewhere your head's
still full of serpents staring each
other down in the arid reflection
you find on the arc of the covenant's
surly gold surface disease realizing
after all this time you've actually
managed at long last   to vampire
vanish   ghost town evaporate
unlucky abduction disappear

caption this conspiracy

outside of history live leftover beachgoers grown enormous

u.s. phony sirs, limiting abductions to cock-&-hen contortion

clones out-droning one another for a brighter slice of startover

sky—*i don't know why they chose me*, but here i lie, my mind

a private raid of needle probes & off-the-grid no-fly zones

seldom pushing daisies past the greenhouse gas & senate

to a god above war's havoc, alien sheiks unleash their

long-holstered hole-punches & puncture the brains of

every radioactive laugh track, humanoid vectors complete

w/ bomb income & quarantined longing, but my wannabe

song doesn't get very far, once a droid & porn starlet

pair up to destroy it, showing all stabs at leak stop-

page doomed to prove futile, for this brutal moonlight

outfit's always been about the eyelets—now let me

tell how to explain this plain-sight fusion: it involves

a balled-up string, a cuticle, a missile set to *luminate*

worldwide whine

the sun is just diff lately

more thirsty to obliterate me

just take it   just take it   just take it

as it comes around here it's so hot

even in december the christmas trees

strip down to their skivvies

melted popsicle trickles down

the divot in america's midriff

i wanna be a river nymph in south louisiana

forging 1,000 howling voodoo nests

from sticky pinecones caked in sabbath

this delta valley needs my celtic sex

divine spark for itself i know it

swampy harpy catching seedlings

up her stillborn psychic spider web

while meantime along lake michigan

warring factions of the forest thaw

in fevered intervals like choir cues

how can my fellow global locals stand it?

so much homeland left for us to powerstrip

pre-extinction syndrome

crampy packing to go back

to a no-man's ransacked mansion

laughing damp-eyed underground

my abdomen opens up its ancillary

madness masking universal cancers

with the dark fact of devour

wring my seed pod by the neck

watch my whole species leaving

lifeless slime trails down the coastlines

thirsty for the will to drown

measured out in shot glasses

& electroshock therapy blisters

nevermind the fisted distance

trade winds travel to give us hell

nevermind the swell of marshy

sewage looming bootheeled overhead

alphabentitus

psycho junkyard varmints got me magically bat-shit bankrupt
by meat-juice o'clock

like fuck there's nothing left but our asbestos back porch &
fat guest room cigars

on & on   oh no she didn't   roll credits for jesus
rape a rainbow in its sleep

i'm verifying my own virginity w/ a magnifying glass until
the sun starts to burn through

i been thank-you-much baptized in ape shit & jungle funk since
the day i was first misconstrued

i still feel it running out the raging parties of my undies
reefer dens   mushroom hells   lazy

underage keg stand's embarrassing back bend of death
why don't we maypole this day trip

into pagan outer space? like some unstudied workweek rerun of
my favorite sci-fi show on blow

i'm not changing my street name this late in the game
not taking any rides downtown

just to powder my ashes over the village oil can   or snub the
upchuck cuties on the corner

for asking why my robot buttons glow no longer   short answer:
my ALPHABENTITUS JUST DON'T GO THERE

tear my clumsy stunt double   a new uptick esophagus
suck the noxious tusk melt from my slutty mirror skirt

at mid-dock I should have said it   sure as my former den mother
is now an orthodontist   sure as shit is getting out of hand

kiosk cancer

let's say today's a perfect day to polarize your genome
or start looking straight snakebit on your bikini line
how many humans before you have felt their fingernails grow
long while pissing in the dark? the rest is just compost
& taxidermied smiles, the reasons already receding upstream:
that's the dance of a man who thinks he's king of something
like initiating makeup sext over gchat when you leave him
the champagne of tall babies, 24 oz. on his doorstep
so that to activate the pull tab apparatus he is forced
to perform a lip reader's wet dream, imaginary bestie mum-
mified in gauzy fog & weeds, except—scandal!—there's nothing
underneath but the elaborate screen saver of your reproductive
chemistry—shh, please wait until surgery is adjourned
before ordering more kiosk cancer as seen on tv round the world

no hard line

knife hits at nightfall, key bumps before bed
why the ruby you gave me turned black w/ forget
as if neither of us had ever been born enough
to claim a monthly stone for weighing down
our ancestors' ghosts—meanwhile i'm getting
so high somebody asks whether i have a
lazy eye—how else to reply but w/ a lie?
tell the devil how to buy the next election
hate to break it to you, kid, but this one's
sans exception: the dead don't just come
back by bacteriological suggestion but
linger in the embers until the fire single-files
out your billfold into silence, no hard
line between my heaving titties & your
deviated sinus, no fighting all the thirst
we burst to quench w/ burning leaves &
ancient powdered remedies passed down
passed out from screen to shining screen

bb murderer

can i wish on this? baby
murderer hissed, first nightmare
vision howling out his bowl of
ice cream, but all he hears is the
i-scream you-scream of the we-all-
scream spinning galaxy turning his
spitball rosebud red—what if the
heavens never said or set in stone
hard & fast rules about something
as fever-natural as death? or what
if mr. godhead said it, but then lived
to regret & STET it like *what-
ever's clever, i've killed scores
of endangered angels yet i'm not
condemned a felon.* desperate
for that power tantrum, baby
downs the last of his sweet
snack, smacking satisfied lips
on severed limbs still scared
too stiff   to snap

money / talk

thank you to the IRS for threatening
to fine my ass, for giving me a reason
explicable in psychopathic-speak to
call my mother, say *dear god i have
a problem only a bible-thumping
anorexic songbird can resolve*
and it has to do with some number
of shekels buried in the ground
has to do with the quantity of baby
teeth you saved inside a valentine—
red ribbon wrapped around—the
trouble with me is i'm turning to
rubble, the trouble is you lined my
childhood bed too many times with
vicodin & lemon trees run wild. *oh
the pill it is bitter but the numbing
power is sweet!* no straight & narrow
just hard 180's, extremist to the marrow
whether apocalyptic harlot or the soldier
of a saintly light, one day evolution knew:
your automatic drafty laugh advantaged
you, a pathos pathology squanders unsaid
i'm helping myself—excuses, excuses
—excuse myself from having nothing
left to say to you but what the tax
collectors tell me to

god complex

in the reliquary fairy dust
i feel see-thru
like father, like fortune

i hope my coffin comes
w/ built-in glory-holes
yes plural, yes poisoned

w/ the tears of dead saints
celibate soulmates
happy to hate, happy to castrate

this gravy train of grave mistakes
i call my shoddy rotting bod
a god forgotten, a god in bed

but out the door by 5 AM
maybe my ghost-shame
shoulda waited, shoulda stayed

w/ bated breath, but what's
the pleasure in telepathy
w/o a wall, w/o a distance met?

sad factory

my child-sized pain spout leaks like the saddest factory

matchmaker matchmaker make me unlatch my baby

brainpan from its thirst for a caretaker who doesn't

ache to shake me into syndrome b/c by now home

isn't home w/o a break so bad you see the bone

so alone out in the open w/ no muscle or blood

vessels to soften the blow of womb's afterglow

sun hung so low you might think it fish bait for

the overgrown globe coaxing locust-fed toddlers

back into the water, like *don't you remember*

your invertebrate mother stoning your tentacled

velum to sleep?

headless rain

the sun gargles its daily flareful
of special-needs spray paint

shelters tie-dyed deserter soldiers
inside long-silent grand pianos

in time, when all the planets align
and my pink cud starts to stink just right

the high-wire becomes cosmological
no-no, faux pas of the *almost*

died variety, eyeballing me seductively
from the far side of the galaxy

nice to know another ghost vibrates
at the same ache, the same superhighway

of headless rain, adorning my sugar body
in vulgar shades of vandalize & snowmelt assassinate

medicine manhole

terminal dizzy

previously on my dick...
i thought of everything and then thought better of it

my placebo costume squeaked out the national anthem
b4 a ballgame where my slut-shame reached *arrest me* levels

let's level the playing field like demolition derbies dent the sky
if i were the sky i'd climb out of my car screaming, *what are*

all you humans fucking blind? i'm just sitting here minding my
own nitrogen when your wartime strife spears me in the eye

demanding an afterlife—well alright, your wish is my demise
please find your desired hellfire shining out the earth's bipolar

asshole—too bad we're too busy banging it out to remember
our safe word is a mermaid whose pussy rains down caviar on

the subway terminal, dizzy w/ modernity's cock-tease disease
yes we've converted our body heat into steam, but next episode

who will be left here to power the beast-machine?

suddenly i might believe in chakras and shit

dearest bleary plastic memory, remember when my childhood
dentist obtained that ever-entertaining waiting room game
where you focus all your brain power on dragging heavy metal
marbles via magnet, fighting gravity through glass? my sister
asked, *how dare you thwart me, holy force field?* the seething
barrier between press & release, water & steam, whatever feels
like make-believe until it sticks to your intestines for keeps
in 1923, my irish matriarch swears she could see the poison
berries bulging black inside her little brother's belly the day she
couldn't make it home from school in time to say goodbye
so the following april she matriculated into child labor
a factory of girlish fantasies gone sour, gouging needles under
thumbnails, but unlike the hungry youngest, her other brothers
died w/ world war honor and her only child, born of rape, came
out breech with bad knees so that all the way through this
working-class reverie she might dream to be translucent like a
medicated angel or the way we think of doomed bubonic plague
prey—filled with fruit

S.A.D.

when caked in flesh-eating booze-infused mascara i wake up next to a
moaning unicorn w/ morning wood, i fast-track bargain-bin my sins
for cash, mashup auto-tuned samplings of several former selves
start foaming ghostly at the blessed yuletide girdle, pull my
skirt up and say *cheese!* to the dirty fester underneath
down south at the sound of a werewolf howl the
leaves just turn brown and fall down, no majesty
of multicolored myth-mas reaper, the reason
my sleepy never-before-seen steed has sea-
sonal affective demons fiending for a bright-
er phenome, bites the hand that feeds him
insect feelers & b&w nostalgia propaganda
take a gander at what the nationalist in-
stitute for scientific violence would give
to monitor this bad boy's orgasm—go
ahead, tell me what i should ask for
in exchange for a stolen specimen
give me a # 1 to a million
give me the secrets of
the universal side-
show turned to
petri-ridden
trash

novel idea

novel idea: in which every line of dialogue, internal and external, is ascribed to "nobody, ever"

novel idea: in which pilgrim makes no progress, but waits for godot all alone just like the rest of us

novel idea: in which every chapter ends with an increasingly elaborate suicide, like that grand theft auto-asphyxiated dream but on repeat precisely nine times, like felines fall from treetops yet somehow kindly decline to die

novel idea: in which i've really been a funeral pyre this entire time

novel idea: in which solipsism turns out to be true, but only for one minor character, so that when s/he's struck by a city bus the world shuts off with a quiet *blip!* like a 50's television swallowing its final wad of bunny-eared spit

novel idea: in which i'm running out of novel ideas already and it's only act II with one shoe still stuck in my childhood injury suit

novel idea: in which our hero is reincarnated as a red wheelbarrow but still can't understand what that damn poem meant, and in not understanding understands better than any college professor can

novel idea: in which a poet tries to write a novel, spends 10 long years tonguing the muses' clits, and when s/he's finished swings a lasso overhead bc that's how far out s/he'd like to drag this callow rag—so high it might just count as divined archive by the time it beams back down

cyborgs sigh too

under a cartoon rain cloud my
motherboard fries crispy golden
inside, dripping sweet crude lime-
lit moonshine all over its primitive
pretty-girl circuits hissing fits oh
so ludicrous lovely i know i'm alive
for no other reason than to survive
the world's final bad-man unmask
disguised as surprise sinus infection
or those mistletoe traditions fistfuls
of sinister x factor hide behind
no, i'm not exactly "fine" but
receiving the sky's permission
to die is its own kind of high
quixotic finder's fee tonight
for a child-sized flying saucer
of what makes machines scream

submissive's song

in the fists of impossible monsters
this is what the future bites like
all dappled in broken blood vessels
& the angry ash of hazmat have-nots

take it from the shoestring-limp sub-
missive who knows: those who aren't
experienced in daddy's belt tightening
about the neck might do best to avoid

un-sun-goggling their eyes in front of
close friends. *what's that violent-edged*
corona radiating down your lash line?
and you won't intuit how to tether

their worry to your pleasure, won't
coerce yourself to say what evanesces
in a chokehold: the not-yet-severed
dungeoning in someone else's ample hands

i see right thru you to the real you who is also see-
thru

down to the lobster bother trapped inside your pelvis

selfish maybe to sneak a boil, to spoil your virgin shell

w/ seaweed smeared in the sewer drain's prosthetic rainfall

go call on your bevy of seven crows in rome, phone a friend

w/ prophetic benefits—whatever they tell you

will be just another alphabetic cellulose gone septic

just another muttered *scalpel* you can never stop by saying *uncle*

under the ozone layer of accepted loss

nothing indigenous isn't brimming w/ your froth

first off // best off

first off the boat   in my haute gyroscope
      i charm too hard

marmoset skins   swing me aloft
      six stitches for every

cracked acrylic   shellacked in magic spells
      & shredded benjamins

most of my cost   goes into gaudy
      lingerie, laundry

mats in my hair   self-righteous lice
      lying about getting

laid in the light   of a cursed hermit's halo
      i cry in the shower

so i can't hear you   freak the whole neighborhood
      out w/ your frat-boy

remember-when   erections   could hold
      this whole country up?

remember rolodexes   unprotected sex
      your fave syndicated softcore clone?

nick@nite neon logo   glow? wouldn't you
      take it all back w/ a cackle?

the whole after-school   shit snack? the whole
          coal tunneled thru?

wouldn't you like to   make love to a dinosaur? fondle
          a mastodon? ask adam himself

where his god went   so wrong? first off
          i bent my brother's

harp string til it broke   first off, i think
          i'm on a fucking roll

more often than not   more often than i let myself go
          down a forgetting hole

w/o tracing my name   on some stretch of the threshold
          some record to cover

my dust under   music paper
          made to dance exactly

at the speed of gravity   so we ball it up
          powder/snort it

paint the galaxy white   but sure as every
          good boy does fine

we can never bleach   the color of the night
          the color sentiment

irrevocably renders   double funeral-wide
        for every drug runner

we know full well   was & could be but won't
        now that first off

my acetylene head   first *cough* best *cough*
        can never stay first off for long

millennial masochist

the ghost of x-mas jazz is growing scalpel-tipped wings again
telling me i was forever right on time until i turned 25

when my hive mind lost patience for pop stars, designer
drugs, fight scars, and my dr. informed me tactful

millennial masochists pay the pros the big bones for sterile
needles, just-curious biopsies, exploratory surgeries w/ only

minor high-times pain relief, so i hopped on that bandaged
bandwagon, staggered my breathy screams as he bored

gorgeous molehills into my skull at equal intervals—maybe
it was the vibration but, baby, it felt just like your long lost lover's

stroke, w/ all the blood blocked out the brain and dropping
down into our doll parts parsed out dissected by a moan

belting

but who can know? even in the biblical sense. i made a mirror
out of crows' tongues and goddamn it really glows, like maybe
whatever genetic junk i'm made of is meant to silence singing.
i've been silenced one too many times to sing at full volume in
front of strangers, so now that's how you know you know you
know you know me, when i sing so loud you cower—no no, my
mother called it *belting* like i was the one beating her, a grand
reversal where my oral dexterity takes a break from holding up
the saints' slacks—all day long i'm busy fashioning the fasteners
between us. i say i'll save my voice for jerusalem's next yearend
feast, but then i notice my sad-eyed raft has cocooned into a
grand piano with the strings and pedals still intact, so when i lift
my pagan beach dreads unto heaven, bless the tide, untie my
tongue, i'm belting one world to the next, the eternal yes and
never snuggled up together underneath my dress

etc. etc.

tonight i'll bite the tongue my mother sharpened
but deep down inside my windpipe there's a virus
i can't silence, whining thru diamonds, *i feel ya*

ophelia, the madness becomes us, flushing
pretty/tidal/vibrant w/ traces of violence still
on us at sunset, neck & wrists tied lightly

flower-dainty like, *might break if pressed*
too hard into a page of hungry succubi
gone wild b/c the nurses' aides come for you

sweet ladies, from either side of the asylum
to pry your stitches out by hand, discard the
binding, press your petals up against a lens

say goodnight into the microscope, etc. etc.
no, i can't hear you, say it louder, etc. etc.
don't wait it out, admit we're right, etc. etc.

the drowning ends but then again it doesn't ever

who's to tell

don't concern yourself w/ why i fall
silent in the dime store dressing room

i'm simply considering what the cops
could tell about me from my corpse alone:

twenty-something / female / nailbiter
a ham in the bedroom (groomed pubic hair)

poor circulation / chronic disease / purple knees
eats amitriptyline, cyclobenzaprine, daily b.c.

forever not ready for... next of kin? forget it
just a long procession of indiscretions

one after another, who's to tell whether
she fell in love too easily or not at all?

subliminal scars traverse wrists, shins
chief inspector thinks stigmata, then chokes

back unchewed dogmatism, spewing out
baptismal-like onto the parking lot, rinsing away

all forensic evidence of foul play or wtf
i was last seen trying to say, *choke me*

only hard enough to make the ceiling blur
to make the mad forget their self-inflicted

sores deep inside the drawstring pockets
of the body left to rot outside your door

fucked up firsts

out of my whole palaceful of taxidermied teenage boys
you're my favorite, pissing eternally on the rubber moon
perhaps we never rly landed on the perfect NASA snap-
shot of the kennedy assassin i'm down here wearing as a hat
as if it's just another tourist trap inside my dirty film debut
there's no one actually inside me but a b&w tequila worm
they green-screen the erection in later, pin the tail on the
imaginary friend, play *pretend we were each other's fucked
up firsts,* redeeming the worst virgin daze of our lives
thinking sex on the beach wouldn't hammer sand straight
through my hourglass physique—yes, i see this year
it's chic to misremember, tremor, have too much to drink
but in the long run who will recreate, cosplay the deadbeat
dungeon master w/ his feet up on the back of daddy's seat?

apolitical apology

forgive my sappy paci-fascism, patio drugs pitter-pattering across
the trap-door floor
on optimistic days i start seeing my demons in terms of
dreamscape aerodynamism
an exercise in personally devising flight inside the empty space
behind modernity's
big bad gouged-out eyes, parasites deny themselves happiness
too, just like you

just like the amoeba must have long enough to emerge from its
primordial stew
so much simpler to stay single-celled, this side of hell
quasimodo-cowering
beneath the heavy bells of patriarchy, arching my back to show
l'oréal only my curves
make me worth it, emerging silent from the sideshow three-ring
binder of my spine

ashine w/ virus from on high, i hear the tradewinds shift, god &
the devil kiss
eclipse whatever's left of evolution's short shrift, my own fists
come to enrage me
b/c they shake sans basic facts or calculations, until i hear the
crowd shout for
no more all-inclusive reindeer games! and feel the shame of the
misbehaved slave

caving in at the creamy candy-coated center of the collective
what-have-you
now that i realize my internment is a virtue: *ow you touched me
don't let go*

surrogate somebody

i remember in winter she'd leave the curling iron on at all times
so when i washed my hands the drips would hit in little sizzles or
miss and swish inside the water bed she kept even as a single
mother, even as an avid cat-lover, saving baby rabbits from their
killer jaws at dawn, belting out the shrillest soprano bombast of
phantom, les misérables in the forest   green van w/
bad handling & peeling window tint—just another day in a diva's
life, smiling at the cute pastor, savoring scandal, playing her
scales for the high school chamber choir—maybe someday
someone's queen again, either onstage, under the sheets or
somewhere in between, b/c her once-loving husband left her
for a family friend, and i said *those two deserters deserve each
other* before knowing it was already the talk of the revival tent
before knowing she was already good as dead, but seldom did i
tell a soul what she told me not to tell them then—winking from
her single dilated pupil, smirking from her infamous mole, she
poured me my first glass of kahlúa, and i knew it was working
when i forgot who was who at 15 in the terra cotta kitchen
we could only afford to laugh in as house-sitters

i'm that river too sick to fish

finish w/ a pan-out to all the trashed animals dying to brine in
me, the steamboat gothic marine arena wreathed in black algae
& ragged-edged reefs—perhaps one of their ancestors let its
cold blood run wrong all the way down the evolutionary tree to
me, perhaps that's why my flower stems are growing calculated
scales—pan back in and you'll see me pan-frying in my own juicy
delusions, damned to burn brittle at the corrugated border
where my country touches every ocean w/ its oily prosthesis &
the unconscious cups the deepest waters before spreading its
fingers super   slowmo   over landfill

plantation nation

on a steady diet of progestin & dead progeny
i dream a *gone with the wind* parody in which
the red earth of tara becomes subject to terror
boeing 747 crashes in its own reflection, tumor
ridden twin rabbits sad-screw and then scab over
so many sober speak nows, never hold your peace
still i don't scream when i'm supposed to, frozen
cross-stitched to the scene, a hoop skirt burning
sans inhabitants b/c we can can give a damn about
a pallid heroine w/o both pelvic floor & ceiling caving in
but when the music swells, plantation nation's damned
to hell, there is no tragedy to say befell our southern belle
just paradise propeller-sent while all around we find ourselves
newlywed nude & spewing sacred rainbows onto fields of
unforbidden fruit scorched much too black to blanch

last-gasp applause

look at me, so busy coveting the cantilever of least resistance
i forget to clean the *oh my god* out my shotgun, neglect to crop
the seasick hickey from my cheesy LA headshot, what a shame
to feel ashamed of what we cannot haunt, the slay that made
the dragon wax al dente in his own last-gasp applause—don't
you see there's never been a need to send a crazed knight after
me? i've been vying to dive down this murky spiral staircase half
my life now, to feel the dying of the light whiz by my paralyzed
disguise so *silent night* it gets me high enough to finally feel
wide-eyed alive, shining my fickle bloodshot bullseyes down the
open firing line of the horizon—oh me oh my, this masterpiece
sighs *mistress please*, malinger here inside the forked neck of the
infernal *why* while you can still assign the seven names of satan
to every answer, plastered to the wind three sheets from shore
where the beast still lives, according to lore

sorry not sorry

i hope no liquefied storage terminal can sleep at night
in their groundswell, the ardor deli riots have formally begun

the double-kick drum of the hungry heartspan gagged w/ stones
i love so my throat will fill up with noxious terrible gonging

so my teeth will melt just enough to turn sticky like glue
then the swallows descend w/ their iron lungs & shrugged logic

when birds freeze to death on the streets i wonder why
i'm the only one gawking, sauced & scary-eyed

w/ wispy pink hair standing on end at the end of the world
there is nowhere to put all the soiled rags, nowhere that sags

quite like nature's jagged red teat, but now when we suckle
the rainforest it transmits HIV through its breast milk

strokes our misshapen heads like it's sorry but it's not sorry at all
if my bedsores don't suppurate the junkie guilt of what's
happened   what will?

Notes

Epigraph: from Allen Ginsberg's *Howl*.

p. 1: this section title is stolen (with permission) from Vincent Cellucci's Bywater bar chatter after an installment of Megan Burns' Bloodjet Poetry reading series in New Orleans.

p. 5: "in the face of pain there are no heroes" is drawn from George Orwell's *1984*.

p. 8: "vertigo" and "guernica" reference Hitchcock and Picasso, respectively.

p. 12: "same rat, different hat" is taken from an episode of *Bob's Burgers*.

p. 27-28, 36: several lines from these poems are drawn from YouTube's automatic captions of various alien abduction documentaries.

p. 30-31: this poem was originally written for a collaborative project on overused tropes in big-budget action movies, *Re:ACTION!*

p. 36: the penultimate stanza here alludes to a memory i have of Laura Mullen describing her then-present outfit as "all about the eyelets."

p. 42: "key bumps before bed" is another roguish gem from Mr. Cellucci, and "sans exception" references his "exceptionalist manifesto" in *an easy place / to die*.

p. 44: "the pill it is bitter but the numbing / power is sweet!" is a play on Peter, Paul & Mary's "Lemon Tree."

p. 46: "matchmaker matchmaker make me unlatch" is a play on the *Fiddler on the Roof* song.

p. 47: "special-needs spray paint" is a phrase drawn from a painfully hungover conversation with Jordan Soyka & Veronica Barnes. the context is lost to time.

p. 51, 61: "previously on my dick..." & "the ghost of x-mas jazz" are more Vince-isms.

p. 54, 66, 69: references include *Pilgrim's Progress*, Grand Theft Auto, "The Red Wheelbarrow," *The Hunchback of Notre-Dame*, "Rudolph the Red-Nosed Reindeer," *Gone with the Wind*, and "Black Dark Rainbows" (a poem my friend Nathan Gropp wrote in high school and may be surprised i remember).

p. 63: this poem was written for the late, brilliant, beautiful Michelle Greenblatt, and features a reference to *Hamlet* ("sweet ladies") also featured in "The Wasteland."

p. 67: for Peyton and McKenna, and their mother, Shari Sue Fretz.

p. 71: "the ardor deli riots" was a phrase/concept coined in conversation with Amanda James. context & rightful ownership are again lost to time.

Acknowledgements

Thank you to my parents, my sister Rachel, my aunt Karen, Riley Teeters, Tim Jones, Laura Theobald, Lara Glenum & the entire LSU MFA family, and Vincent Cellucci, whose stream-of-consciousness silliness inspired numerous lines and the first section title of this book, as well as Tom Simmons and Ron Starbuck for believing in this project more than I believed in it myself. Warm thanks are also due to James Leaf, Luis Neer, Jake Syersak, Hilal Omar Al Jamal & Christopher Payne, Jean Vengua, Taylor Gorman, Jessica Rae Bergamino & Laura Bylenok, Jill Khoury, Jonathan Penton & Michelle Greenblatt (R.I.P.)—all editors who helped the following poems first find life in their respective journals:

Alien Mouth ("who's to tell," "fucked up firsts," & "alphabentitus")

Atrocity Exhibition ("automatomic," "over[h]eating," "money / talk," "submissive's song," & "belting")

Cloud Rodeo ("millennial masochist" & "sorry not sorry")

Fine Print ("un-cudgel")

Local Nomad ("no hard line" & "headless rain")

Mojo ("draw one // pick again")

No Assholes ("absence knows best")

Quarterly West ("far cry")

Reality Hands ("plantation nation")

Rogue Agent ("i see right thru you to the real you who is also see-thru")

Unlikely Stories ("ghost porn," "borderline," "committed," "sympathy pill," & "etc. etc.")

Witch Craft ("god complex")

About the Author

Dylan Krieger is a transistor radio picking up alien frequencies in south Louisiana, where she earned her MFA from LSU and now sunlights as a trade magazine editor. Her debut poetry collection, *Giving Godhead* (Delete Press, 2017), won LSU's 2015 Robert Penn Warren Award and was dubbed "the best collection of poetry to appear in English in 2017" by the New York Times Book Review. She is also the author of *no ledge left to love* (Ping Pong Free Press, forthcoming) and an autobiographical meditation on the Church of Euthanasia called *The Mother Wart*. Find her at www.dylankrieger.com.

About the Cover Artist

Rachel Krieger graduated from Columbia College Chicago with a BA in Photography, and continues to be inspired by the city of Chicago and its surrounding landscapes. While at Columbia, she worked as a Teaching Assistant, specializing in 19th century photographic methods and other experimental techniques. Her interests in architecture, history, city planning, and landscape design all contribute to her artistic style, process and subject choices. One of her projects focusing on parks in Chicago and the surrounding suburbs was included in the 2014 BA + BFA Photography Manifest Exhibition. Besides photography, she designs jewelry, and her Black Sun Jewelry line can be found online at blacksunjewelry.etsy.com.

www.ingramcontent.com/pod-product-compliance
Lightning Source LLC
LaVergne TN
LVHW091313080426
835510LV00007B/482